Contents

Words that appear in **bold** are explained in the glossary.

The answers to the questions are on pages 20-21.

Sunlight

Light is a kind of energy that we see with our **eyes**. During the **day**, we get **natural** light from the sun. We call this light **sunlight**.

NEVER look directly at the sun, even if you are wearing sunglasses, because it can damage your eyes.

Sunlight is very **bright** when there are no **clouds**. Bright light helps us to see things easily.

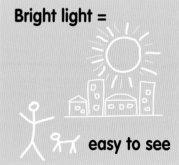

Bright light =

easy to see

Clouds in the sky sometimes block out some of the sunlight.

Dim light

The clouds make the sunlight **dim**, or less bright. Is it easier or harder to see when the light is dim?

5

Darkness

When there is no light, there is **darkness**. It is dark at **night** because one half of our **Earth** blocks out the sun's light from the other half.

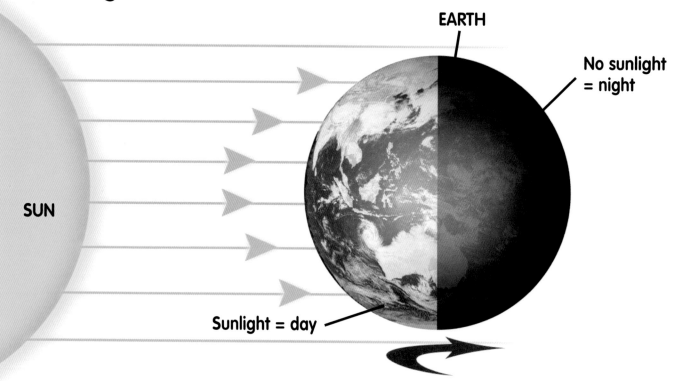

EARTH

No sunlight = night

SUN

Sunlight = day

Earth is a ball that rotates (spins around). It takes 24 hours (or 1 day) to spin all the way round. At any time, half the Earth has sunlight and half is in darkness.

Now it's your turn...

You can block out light with objects that are much smaller than the Earth.

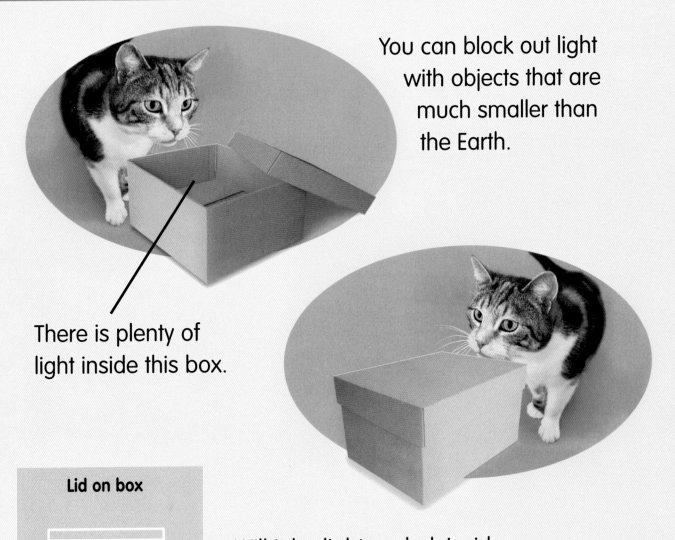

There is plenty of light inside this box.

Lid on box

Will it be light or dark inside the box if you put on a lid?

7

Making light

When it is dark, we can make **artificial light** by switching on an electric lamp or a torch.

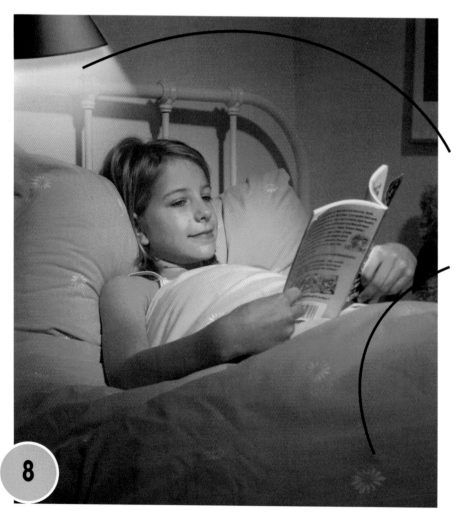

The light is brightest close to the lamp. The light gets dimmer further away from the lamp.

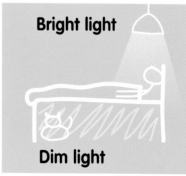

Bright light

Dim light

Now it's your turn...

You can use a torch to read in the dark.

Torch close to page

Is it easier or harder to see
a page in your book if you
hold a torch close to it?

Straight lines

Light travels in straight lines, so we cannot see around corners or over walls.

The dog and cat cannot see each other because the wall blocks any light travelling between them.

Now it's your turn...

Do you think the cat and dog can see each other if the cat jumps up onto the wall?

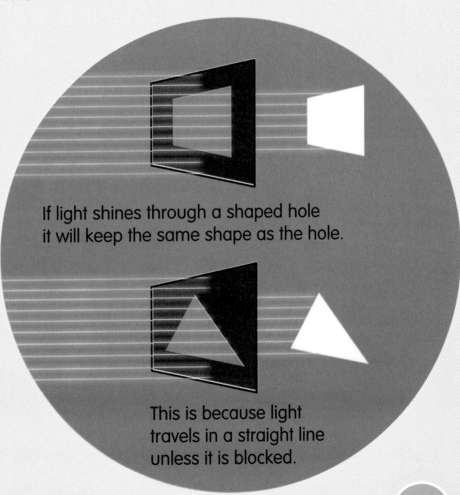

If light shines through a shaped hole it will keep the same shape as the hole.

This is because light travels in a straight line unless it is blocked.

Sound

Sound is a kind of energy that we hear with our **ears**. Sounds can be **quiet** or loud.

Whispering makes a quiet sound. When we whisper we can only be heard by people near to us.

Near = easy to hear

Check it out   Now it's your turn...

Shouting makes a loud sound. We shout when we want someone far away to hear us.

Far away

Hello

Hello

Shouting is very, very loud if you are near to a person. How loud is it if you are far away?

13

Vibrations

Sounds are made of **vibrations** that travel through the **air**. Sounds happen when the air vibrates – shakes backwards and forwards very quickly.

We cannot see the vibrations, but when they reach our ears, we hear sounds.

Vibrations = sounds

Check it out

Now it's your turn...

The boy plucks the guitar strings to make them vibrate and make sounds.

What happens to the sounds when the guitar strings stop vibrating?

No vibrations

15

Making sound

When objects move or bang together they usually make sound.

Hitting the top of the drum makes it vibrate and produce sound. Hitting the drum gently makes a quiet sound.

A gentle hit = a quiet sound

Now it's your turn...

What do you think happens to the sound if you hit the drum harder?

A hard hit

BANG!

BANG!

17

Heard but not seen

Sound travels through the air in a different way to light. Sound is not as easy to block as light.

This mother cat cannot see her kitten around the corner, but she can hear it miaowing.

You can often hear things that you cannot see.

Miaow

Now it's your turn...

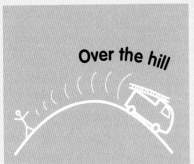

Over the hill

Will you still be able to hear this fire engine's siren when the fire engine goes around a corner or over a hill?

19

Answers

Page 5

It is harder to see when the light is dim. Bright light is better for seeing.

Dim light =
harder to see

Page 7

It will be dark inside the box because the lid blocks out all the light.

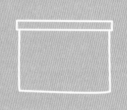

Lid on box =
no light in box

Page 9

It is easier to see the page in the dark if you hold the torch close to the book.

Torch close to
page = easier
to see

Page 11

If the cat is on the wall, the cat and dog can see each other in a straight line.

Cat on top of
wall = dog can
see cat

Page 13

The shouting will be quiet, because even loud sounds are quiet if you are far away from them.

Far away = harder to hear

Page 15

The sounds stop when the guitar strings stop vibrating.

No vibrations = no sounds

Page 17

Hitting the drum harder, with increased force, produces louder sounds.

A hard hit = louder sounds

Page 19

You can still hear the fire engine, even when it goes around a corner or over a hill.

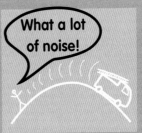

Over the hill = heard but not seen

Glossary

air A mixture of gases that are all around us on the Earth's surface.

artificial light Light that is made by humans.

bright Strong light that is easy to see.

clouds Clusters of water droplets that float in the air.

darkness When there is no light.

day Period of daylight from morning to evening.

dim Weak light that is difficult to see.

Earth The planet where we live. It is a huge, spinning, ball-shaped rock.

ears The parts of the body that humans and animals use for hearing.

eyes The parts of the body that humans and animals use for seeing.

light A kind of energy that we see with our eyes.

natural Made by nature.

night Period of darkness from evening to morning.

quiet Faint sounds that are difficult to hear.

shouting Speaking very loudly.

sound A kind of energy that we hear with our ears.

sunlight Natural light that comes from the sun.

whispering Speaking very quietly.

vibrations When something shakes backwards and forwards, or from side to side, very quickly.

23

Index

Picture credits

t=top, b=bottom, c=centre, l=left, r=right, OFC=outside front cover
Corbis: 1, 3, 4, 5, 10, 11, 14, 15, 18, 23. Powerstock: OFC, 2, 7, 8, 9, 12, 13, 16, 17, 19

Every effort has been made to trace the copyright holders, and we apologise in advance for any unintentional omissions. We would be pleased to insert the appropriate acknowledgements in any subsequent edition of this publication.